The
Professor

Finding Faith, Education, Joy

JEFF IRELAND

authorHOUSE®

AuthorHouse™
1663 Liberty Drive
Bloomington, IN 47403
www.authorhouse.com
Phone: 1 (800) 839-8640

Published by AuthorHouse   01/12/2018

ISBN: 978-1-5462-2345-0 (sc)
ISBN: 978-1-5462-2344-3 (e)

Library of Congress Control Number: 2018900083

Print information available on the last page.

Scripture taken from The Holy Bible, King James Version. Public Domain

Dedicated to:

Arlene

CONTENTS

The best philosophies evolve from experiences that change the way we think. There is practical philosophy in the story of a life well-lived. A good story should have a lasting effect as well as being a good read. This book is like that."

Dave Sheely

PREFACE

Well, you are now about to read my latest effort to touch people who read through my writing. There was virtually no research that took place while I was writing this book. As the saying goes, this one "came from my gut"! It all started when I decided to sit down and compile a list of 50 acronyms I have written over the years. I used the acronym list to create sentences and paragraphs which eventually morphed into chapters 2, 3, and 9 of this book. These core chapters were the foundation, and the storyline was quick to follow. In writing the storyline, I knew I wanted it to contain a sprinkle of my thoughts on success and a strong element of faith. My faith has gotten me though many difficult times in life, including my most recent and most challenging life crisis which happened in the middle of writing this book. I had my 4th and worst heart attack in August of this year. My heart completely stopped one Sunday evening while playing tennis on a court in Huntersville, NC. I was actually dead for 19 minutes! Thanks to a miraculous touch from the Lord, many wonderful people, and innovative medical technology, I am sitting here today typing this to you. You certainly know, of course, it was the Lord who saved me! Did I see the Lord when I died? I believe I did, but that is a different story and another possible book down the road. I am not sure where life has me heading at this point. I can only say I am so glad to still be on this earth and have had the ability to finish this work. I truly believe things happen for a reason, and I know there are many reasons I am still here. Those reasons will prayerfully unfold as I move forward in my life and continue to grow in my faith. I truly believe one reason was to finish this book. I hope somewhere along the line, with the Lords' help, this book will end up in a person's hands who reads it, and it changes their life in a positive way. I sincerely hope you enjoy the book and the story enclosed.

Jeff Ireland

CHAPTER 1

The Beginning

I am not sure why I stopped. I was a little worn out from running but nothing more than usual. I was running to stay in shape since the swimming season was coming up. As I wound my way up into "the quad", I had this strange urge to stop and rest on the bench. It was a beautiful day with blue skies and snow-white cumulus clouds gently floating by, the kind kids study and imagine they see all kinds of things. It is rare in the Carolinas to have those clouds, since we don't have the moisture like in Minnesota or Michigan with all their lakes. As I ran up to the bench, there he was, not really doing anything just staring up at the clouds. He had a shock of pure white unruly Einstein-like hair and a gentle smile.

"Good afternoon young lady."

"Good afternoon to you too." I replied.

"Running for fun or are you in training?" He inquired.

"Oh, I'm on a swim team here at the school. You have to train year-round if you are going to be any good at it." I responded.

"And are you any good at it?" he asked

"Well… I don't know. I guess I am, I try hard anyway."

"Hmm. You know, you should be more positive in your thoughts on the matter, in all matters actually! You can't approach things with an indifferent attitude, not if you want to succeed." He stated flatly.

I was a little taken back by his directness and I looked at him closer. Was he a grumpy old man or did he have something more to offer?

"Pretty day out, isn't it?" For some reason I felt the need to continue the conversation. I guess I wanted to find out which he was. "What brings you here to the quad today?"

"Oh, just sitting here watching the clouds and using my imagination; two of my favorite pastimes when I am not working." He smiled again as he looked my way. The sun peeking through the clouds gave his face a warm glow.

"So, what do you do when you are working?" I inquired.

"Teach, I am always teaching!"

"Here?" I asked rather startled. In my three years here, I had never seen him around.

"Sometimes yes, but I sort of float where I am needed. You see I am what most people would call retired and just sort of a work freelancer. Feldoar Sooncrae." he smiled and offered his hand, "but everybody calls me "Professor".

"Nice to meet you, Professor Sooncrae" I said as I shook his hand. "My name is Crechette Court."

He nodded, "Nice to meet you Crechette, and not to correct you, but it is just 'Professor'."

"Swimming is a great sport that will help you in a career and family and life in general" he continued.

"Well, all sports do that, don't they? They teach you discipline, commitment and team work?" I replied.

"Yes and no. All sports teach you those lessons, but swimming is different. It's not only a team sport but an individual sport too. Even though you are on a team, you swim against yourself," he replied.

"Well, I don't know about that; you are actually swimming against several people and when you get to a multi team meet you swim against scores of other people." I wondered if this man had ever been to a swim meet.

"Exactly," he said, "and in life, you compete to succeed with life and your career. The illusion is that you are competing against others, but you're really competing against yourself." he said smiling. "Are you first every time you swim?"

"No, not every time. Sometimes I win the heat I am in, but I have never taken a first at a tournament, if that is your question." I added.

"It is my question. And you will note that most tournaments have different winners. In swimming there may always be someone stronger, quicker, and better. If not that particular week, then maybe the next. Of course, prodigies may hold records that may not change for years or decades, but you'll find in sports, rules change, so the record breaker has an asterisk, so to speak."

"Ok, I'll bite, how is swimming more related to life than other sports?" I responded.

"Because in life, when you compare yourself to others you are bound to come up short. In swimming you work to better YOUR times, compare yourself to yourself. As long as you are improving, you should feel good about where you are going. Life is like that. People want to be a success, but compare themselves to others and their accomplishments. I have an acronym for success that I think explains it well. You are familiar with what an acronym is aren't you?"

"Of course, it is a phrase or thought that is boiled down into a word or words where the initials spell out the whole thought." I replied.

"Correct. So, my acronym for success is this: **S**etting **U**p **C**ontinuous **C**ycles **E**ncompassing **S**elf **S**atisfaction." He looked at me to see if I was following.

"Well ok, but isn't self-satisfaction a selfish way to look at things?" I asked.

"Not if you do it right. First, when you are self-satisfied, you are a better person, sibling, parent, child, friend, boss, or employee. You get the idea. Second, I think I need to change the end of the acronym. I believe it could end: **E**ncompassing **S**piritual **S**ervice. You will never be truly satisfied with who you are until you have a spiritual foundation for your values. The basic intent is to serve your fellow human beings. Every person that I have ever met who is truly satisfied with life and themselves has a spiritual foundation from which to base their thinking, judgment and action. There are many who are looking for material wealth, position, power, popularity or celebrity status. But deep down they KNOW there is something missing, and they are not really satisfied as human beings." He concluded.

"Wow, are you a preacher too?" I blurted out, not thinking and regretting it the minute I said it.

He smiled again. "Well not officially, but in a way. We all should be preachers in a sense. Was it St. Francis that said "'Preach the gospel always and if necessary use words'? I believe we are what we ACT LIKE, and that shines through our true character."

I was slightly uncomfortable with the direction our conversation had taken, but I remained intrigued. I was all cooled off now, so more running was out of the question. I was ready to leave but I was also fascinated by the old man's thoughts and obvious wisdom. "What class are you teaching? I may want to sign up this fall." I asked.

"No official class for me, Crechette, but if you care to stop by my office I would be glad to resume our conversation." He replied.

"Where is your office? I asked. "And do you mind if I bring a couple of close friends with me? (My parents always taught me not to put myself in an uncomfortable or awkward situation if I could help it.) Also, please call me CC, everyone does." I added. I did not think the old man was anything but kind, but better safe than sorry. I knew a couple of friends that might benefit from some of his thoughts.

"You're welcome to bring whoever you like. My office is in the School of Business building on the third floor in the corner. Walk to the right after you go through the hallway door from the main steps and you can't miss it. I'm usually there reading and writing, your visit will more than likely be a welcome break from whatever I am doing at the time." He replied.

I had seen how small and cramped most professors' offices were, so it was no wonder he was spending time outside on a day like this. I couldn't imagine spending a whole day cooped up inside.

"When would be a good time for us to come by, and should we bring anything?" I asked.

"You can stop by most anytime, CC. You may want to bring a pen and paper, or, for you young kids, maybe a laptop or tablet. Isn't that the way they take notes now a days? It was surely nice to meet you and good luck with the swimming," he said as I stood to leave.

"Thanks Professor Sooncrae, that is a great name, by the way. What is the origin?" I asked inquisitively.

He smiled. "Remember it's just 'Professor', and my name's origin would be a great topic for our next visit. Let's save it for then, shall we?"

I nodded and smiled, "I really look forward to it, Professor". I turned and jogged away.

It was hard to explain, but I knew change was coming for me in a big way. My understanding of how life should work was going to be different my senior year. I had a feeling that The Professor was a special teacher indeed, but I had no idea how much he would impact my life and the lives of those around me.

CHAPTER 2

The Office

The next time I saw the Professor was in his office the following week. I had dragged two of my best friends, Lynn Rider and Tom Snow, with me. Lynn was a sweet girl and although she didn't swim, we had a lot in common. She was bolder than me, even a wild child on occasion. She certainly wasn't afraid to say what was on her mind, and often had a unique way of looking at things. Tom and I were old friends. We had a lot in common and a similar view of life and its challenges. I had told them about my strange meeting with the Professor. Neither of them had ever seen him around the campus, but were intrigued and agreed to tag along to our meeting.

We entered the building with School of Business carved on the stone facade above the door. The atrium was wide open and went up three floors with offices and classrooms that circled each floor and overlooked the rich leather chairs and couches below. The stairs were not spiral but zig-zagged with two flights per floor. We walked up the four semi-curved marble staircases to the third floor. At the top we walked through a door called administration. Nobody was sitting at the desk, but we noticed a light coming through the open French doors at the end of the room. The Professor was looking at the wall, and when he saw us he welcomed us in.

"Glad I saw you. I see nobody's at the desk again. If the light is on, it means I'm here. I don't always hear so well, so just walk right in."

We moved into the office space and were amazed. "Wow… this is a fantastic office you have, professor." I stammered.

"SWEET!" was Lynn's first word. Tom stepped back outside, then reentered with a soft "Unbelievable" although I knew what he meant was "impossible".

We had all been in professor's offices before, but this office was like stepping into another universe. The wall the professor was looking at was really a library that went floor to ceiling with a ladder on a rail to reach the shelves. It was a deep rich stained wood that matched the trim work throughout the office. To the right of the library walls was a spiral staircase, but instead of reaching another floor, it led to a small landing with a recliner and a reading lamp. Under the staircase was a narrow passage way that ended with a dart board.

In the middle of the room, in front of a gas fireplace, was a beautiful mahogany table that was actually a backgammon game board. It was the most beautiful thing I had ever seen. Every other arrow on the board was one of Jesus' 12 disciples. The beautiful dove flying in the middle of the board was made of stained glass. It simply took my breath away. Above the fireplace was a world map that covered the wall, it was circa 1700's and Greek, based on the writing on it.

"CC, who are your friends?" the Professor offered his hand.

"Lynn Rider" Lynn smiled and beat me to the punch as usual. "Tom Snow", Tom said, as he looked around the room, still amazed. They all shook hands.

"Well it is very nice to meet you both I am Feldoar Sooncrae but please simply call me Professor".

"I'm sorry, but…" I began

"I think we were just taken aback by your office." Lynn continued. "I've never really seen anything like it." Tom finished.

"Well I like it, sort of suits me, I don't think it is for everybody but it is my little place of solace away from the hustle and bustle, so to speak. It's a place to come and think, something most of us don't do anymore."

He smiled as he spoke. "This is a good place to write and research."

He moved behind the most unusual desk we had ever seen. It was made of free form slabs of wood. The top was a footprint shape and the front had a big knot in it that looked like an eye. It was made of old growth red wood with beautiful color and grain patterns. He looked comfortable behind it, as he slid into his red leather chair.

"Please pull up the backgammon chairs and have a seat."

"Professor, thank you seeing us. I was fascinated by our last conversation and wanted to learn more if you have a few minutes." CC began.

He smiled "Not a problem. That's why I extended the offer. I'm glad you brought some friends. It's always good to share, and as you work on this project, you can help each other out. So where did we leave off?"

Feldoar Sooncrae

"So, Professor, I'm intrigued by your name and you mentioned it had a special meaning." I said. "You had promised to share with me when we met."

"Yes, I suppose that is a good place to start. You see, you can't be a success at anything until you can emulate my name!" he said. "That, plus getting the formula and your mind set in order."

All three of us glanced at each other and rolled our eyes. "What do you mean by 'emulate your name'?"

"When you understand the root of the name, it begins to make sense."

"You see my Great-great grandfather was traveling with the Lewis and Clark expedition back in 1804 when it all began. Things went fairly well as they interacted with over 2 dozen Indian tribes along the way. When they first met the Sioux Indians it was not good. It was a hostile meeting and my Great-great Grandfather Levi Barlow was captured and held hostage by the Sioux. Chief Kohana (which meant swift to action) ordered him tortured. They subjected him to unspeakable torture for several days. One of the acts was pulling out the hair on his face and body one by one. However, through it all he never showed emotion, or fear, only his faith in God. Chief Kohana was so moved by his gutsy mentality and his obvious faith he ordered the torture to stop and ordered him to be nursed back to health. While being nursed back to health he fell in love with the girl who had been taking care of him. He stayed with the tribe and Chief Kohana allowed them to be married. Chef Kohana then named him Sooncrae which meant "without fear". He finished.

"Wow, that is kind of romantic" Lynn said. She surprised me, since she doesn't come across as being romantic at all.

"Yes, I suppose it is but more important is the lesson of the name, 'have no fear'."

"Well, I am not afraid of anything. I have no fear!" Tom boasted, puffing his chest in pride. Lynn agreed and I of course nodded as well. "Yeah professor, what is there to be afraid of?"

"Well, the biggest challenge in life is that people convince themselves there is no negativity. That said, we all have fear in varying degrees. However, let's not rush into things. We'd better pace ourselves, if you are all good with that," he said.

Of course, we agreed. Then Lynn asked, "So, what are you talking about?"

He smiled and replied, "Let's have a few meetings and talk about what motivates you in life. We may take different avenues, but we all follow the same motivations, because we are all people!"

"Then we'll talk about how our minds work. Our mental status is critical in all we do. We can discuss climbing the pyramid and how that affects our potential for success. Of course, you never know what else could pop into your brains along the journey!" he concluded.

"Let's start with your view of yourself."

Personal Vision

"What is your personal vision? By that I mean, what do you trust?"

"Actually, we're willing to trust you, Professor. We were just talking about it a couple of days ago and it sounds like we could learn a lot from you" Tom responded.

"Well, it's terrific that you are willing to trust so quickly. Now do you three know what trust actually is?" the Professor responded.

All three looked at each other slightly puzzled, but I jumped on that one.

"I'm pretty sure if you look it up in the dictionary, it is reliance on integrity and strength. A confident perception of something or someone." I was always good at definitions.

Lynn jumped in, "I have a hunch you are going somewhere else with it, right Professor?" She said slyly.

"So, trust means something else to you Professor?" Tom asked.

"Not really, but let's look at it slightly different. I know you learn better when you remember so I have found that there is a great way to not only remember, but also define things. I like to use acronyms, so let's look at this in acronym form."

"Acronym form? I'm not sure I follow you on that Professor!" Lynn jumped in.

"Think of it as taking a complex thought and turning it into a word that is easier to remember!" He replied. "As a matter of fact, let's start with the word acronym, **ACRONYM** = **A**lways **C**onsider **R**eal **O**pportunity **N**ow (in) **Y**our **M**ind". He was smiling again.

All three looked at each other, arching their eyebrows and smirking.

I spoke first. "It sure is a different way of looking at things, but what in the world does that have to do with building trust?"

"Pretty much everything. Let's define **TRUST**. In acronym form, the **T** stands for **T**ruth, because trust comes from honesty and openness with the people you associate with. The **R** is **R**espect. Mutual respect is the foundation on which trust is built! To accomplish that, **U** is **U**nderstanding of others and their differences.

We all approach things differently. There isn't always necessarily right and wrong - just differences. That's why you need to respect other's views. **S** stands for **S**upport. Even if you don't completely agree with a decision or the direction things are moving, your support keeps a team strong. No individual can always be number one if they expect the team to succeed. The **T** stands for **T**ime. **TRUST** takes time. It is an ebb and flow of interactions that develops as we watch how others respond."

"Wow, Professor, that's a lot to take in!" Tom exclaimed.

Lynn and I were both nodding our heads when Lynn said "I guess that would be an easy way to remember a lot of things once you got used to it."

I quickly added "Yeah, do you have any others that would help us remember things, especially ones that could help us in school?"

"Well of course I have others, but you need to understand how your life and your actions so far have impacted you. It helps if you totally understand this concept." He took a slow sip of his coffee, then continued:

"I VALUE LUCK and SUCCESS. AN ACTION SYSTEM with COURAGE and BOLD GUTS, DAD's **GIFT TO ME!"** he said smiling.

"What?" we all said nearly in unison.

"You're telling me my success depends on my dad?" Lynn said. Tom was still stumbling over his response.

"Did you forget what we were talking about? Acronyms. All of the words are acronyms. If you understand the acronyms, you will understand how to be successful."

"OK, I have to hear this 'action system'. Would you explain, please?" Lynn was leaning forward.

"Let's start with **I VALUE**: **I**=Intelligently – **VALUE** = **V**isualize **A**ction **L**ead (by) **U**nderstanding **E**xpectations. That is a powerful statement by itself. You use your intelligence to understand what people expect from your actions, so you can move forward. If you don't understand what others want or need, the results are usually disappointing. It's kind of a drive-thru theory of understanding."

He paused, waiting to for someone to jump in. I did. "What in the world is the drive-thru theory of understanding?"

"What happens when you place an order at the drive-thru? What does the person taking the order always do?"

"They repeat your order back to you!" Tom piped in.

"Exactly, to communicate clearly with people, you simply repeat what you heard back to them. That way you can get clarification and better understand their expectations. This is even more important when someone says something that upsets you. Often, what you understood is not what they meant. Clarification saves anger and hurt feelings."

"Simply cool!" Lynn chimed in.

LUCK - SUCCESS

"OK, so we value luck, success: **LUCK** = **L**aboring **U**nder **C**orrect **K**nowledge, **SUCCESS** = **S**etting **U**p **C**ontinuous **C**ycles **E**ncompassing **S**elf **S**atisfaction. Let's start with luck. Just understand that you will only truly achieve something through labor. No matter what job you do, to succeed you need to put in the work. Although, one man told me he only worked half days, and was extremely successful." Looking at their puzzled faces, he continued. "The way he explained it was '6:00 am to 6:00 pm; I work the first half of the day and the rest of the time I get to do what I want.' Success in life takes time and labor, you have to work for what you want."

"Along the way, you need **LUCK**. If you **L**abor **U**nder **C**orrect **K**nowledge you will continue to learn as you go. It's sad that most people feel that their education ends with graduation. In truth, your education only ends when you die. So, listen, read, experience, experiment and above all, learn. It is critical to your success".

"Well Professor, I know we talked about it before, but how do you define success?" I asked.

"I really have no idea what success is for you three."

All three of them looked shocked and disappointed.

"You see, YOU need to define what success is for YOU! That is the purpose of the acronym, and the key to it is SELF SATISFACTION. What makes you happy? No one can decide that but you. What do you love to do? What do YOU want to do in your heart? That is where you need to focus. Many people go through life trying to impress others instead of following their dreams."

"They define success by where they live, what they drive, and how much money they make. True happiness never comes from those things. It comes from what is in your heart. Many people appear successful, but are unhappy because their dreams faded away while they were busy trying to impress other people."

"It doesn't matter where you live or work as long as you are doing what you love and are not in debt doing it. Debt cancels happiness. So, live the way that you want in a way you can afford to live, doing what you love to do. It doesn't get any simpler than that." He concluded.

"So, what does the continuous cycle part of the acronym mean?" Lynn asked

"Great question. What happens when you set a goal and reach it? Do you sit back and relax or will you set another goal?"

"You set another goal, of course," Tom volunteered.

"Right, most people are happiest when they are working toward a goal. Like plants, if you aren't growing you are dying."

"Is that what you mean by "an action system?" Tom asked.

AN – ACTION SYSTEM

The Professor nodded "Yes indeed, **AN ACTION SYSTEM**: **AN** = **A**lways **N**eed. **ACTION** = **A**ttitude **C**onsistent **T**enacity **I**ntegrity **O**ptimism **N**ow. **SYSTEM** = **S**ighting **Y**our **S**uccess **T**hrough **E**motional **M**otivation.

Let's talk about action. Start with Attitude, it is the most important thing a person needs. There was a study done years ago by the Andrew Carnegie Institute with thousands of people and here is what they found: Your success depends roughly 7% on your knowledge; your education. 12% of your success depends upon how you apply that knowledge, your 'skill-set'. Fully 81% of your success depends on your ATTITUDE. The study has been repeated many times and the results are always similar."

"What about when bad things happen or you are treated unfairly?" I asked.

"You can feel sorry for yourself, or you can take a lesson from the experience."

"So, you think there is a reason for everything Professor, even bad things?" This was a different approach for me.

"When things happen that aren't good or as planned, that is where the Consistent Tenacity comes in. Tenacity is holding fast and persevering, doing the right thing, and you must be Consistent in your values, like your Integrity. At times, associates may cut corners because "no one will notice". But understand this, once you throw your integrity away it will be nearly impossible to get it back. If you want to sleep well at night, don't lie, cheat, fudge numbers or do anything morally wrong. It will weigh on your brain in a very negative way. Finally, do something! Take action Now. Don't say "I have always wanted to do that". DO it!! Don't put things off just because circumstances are not going like you planned."

"Wow, now that was a heavy word Professor!" Lynn piped in.

The Professor smiled, "Now you know how important I believe Action is. It works with the System. Sighting Your Success comes through goals you want to accomplish. I already mentioned that it takes Action.

The other half is Through Emotional Motivation. It is important to do things you want to do and love to do so you can be emotionally motivated to accomplish them."

"In the beginning, to learn the system, you should target small goals so you learn what achievement and success mean. It's important to win a few early on so you know what a great feeling you get when you achieve them. If all our goals are huge and long term in nature, you won't find the rhythm of achievement and that is so important."

"OK" Tom jumped in. "This is pretty amazing and I'm already in over my head, but what in the world is the rest of the sentence for?"

"I'm glad you asked, but are you sure I am not driving you kids crazy?" The Professor looked closely at our faces. "Why don't we continue this discussion next week? If you try to take too much in at once, you're sure to lose some of it."

Reluctantly, we agreed, and planned to meet the following Thursday. All during the next week, as we passed each other on campus, we'd toss acronyms at each other. I'd say "Luck", and Tom or Lynn would respond with "Action" or "Truth." So, when Thursday finally arrived, we were definitely ready.

CHAPTER 3

Courage – Bold Guts

On Thursday, we met outside the School of Business and headed up to the Professor's office. He looked up from the book he was reading, smiled, and welcomed us warmly. "Come in. Come in. It's wonderful to see you. I was just doing a little studying myself."

"You were studying?" Tom asked. "Why?"

"Because you are never done learning, not if you want to remain relevant. Every so often in your life, you should look back and see how much your thinking has changed as a result of what you've learned. Now, where were we?"

"We were working on **AN ACTION SYSTEM**." Lynn volunteered.

"Ah yes", the Professor recalled. One important thing to remember about **AN ACTION SYSTEM** is that it needs to be done with **COURAGE** and **BOLD GUTS**."

"What?" We chorused.

"Well to be honest with you, there is no acronym for "with", but the sentence would not make sense without the word," he said chuckling. "With that said, **COURAGE** = **C**oncentration **O**n **U**nderstanding **R**eal **A**ctual **G**rind **E**nthusiastically.

BOLD GUTS = **B**asic **O**ptimism **L**oyal **D**ecisive - **G**et **U**nique **T**enacity **S**atisfied."

"Let's start with Courage. I know you are always taught that, courage is important, and it is, but this is a little different way of looking at it. Concentration, in this world is critical! We are too distracted by emails, texts, snap chats, TV news. We get blasted by what is going on around us non-stop and it is easy to lose focus on your goals. It is also easy to tell ourselves 'oh we will get to it later'. You must **C**oncentrate **O**n what you are trying to accomplish."

"The challenge each and every day is **U**nderstanding, and for the most part it seems like a **R**eal **A**ctual **G**rind. Not only our lives, but our jobs bring us the same type of challenges and distractions. It grinds on us and seems extremely repetitive, so it's no wonder we are glad when Wednesday comes and we are half way through the week. We love it when it's finally Friday, so we gear up for our weekend.

The crucial point on the courage end is the last word **E**nthusiastically. You need to approach whatever God sends your way with enthusiasm weather it is positive, negative, repetitive, routine or something very new. Be enthusiastic and positive in your thoughts and actions as you go along."

"But what if we don't like what's happening to us?" asked Lynn.

"Oh, you don't have to like everything about your life, just don't feel like you have no say in it. Your attitude will determine how things will turn out for you."

I had to think about that, so I made a note to myself.

"On Bold Guts, it is a little bit different, so you may want to pull out some paper from those back packs and jot this one down." The Professor said.

All three of us grinned and looked at each other. "Well Professor" I said, "Not sure you noticed, but all three of us have been grabbing and tapping on our phones on and off while you have been talking!"

"Well as a matter of fact I did notice that," the Professor replied. "I just assumed you were texting friends about our conversation."

Now we all laughed out loud, "No, Professor, all of us have been taking notes on our phones. It's just easier that way. We value your guidance. None of us would be texting while we're learning from you."

The Professor seemed pleased. "Ok, then let's discuss this. Each letter contains three bullet points and all are pretty self-descriptive so I won't spend much time on details. You will get the picture.

B = **B**asics:

1. Dress Right – Be professional in all you do. Dress appropriately and don't be too casual.

2. Be on time – All the time. Everyone's time is valuable so being late is not only unprofessional, it's disrespectful to those you are meeting. Be early to your appointments always.

3. Show Respect – You will encounter people you do not get along with and don't agree with in life and in business. That is ok, but show courtesy and respect regardless. You don't need to be friends to show respect.

O = **O**ptimism:

1. Avoid negative thoughts. Remember that successful people always look at the positive side of every situation.

2. Look for the silver lining. Bad or challenging things will happen but each one contains something we can learn from if we take the time to search for it.

3. Speak to people positively. It is always to your benefit when people think of you as a positive person.

L = **L**oyal:

1. Be Loyal to God

2. Be Loyal to Family

3. Be Loyal to your talent, your skill set and your job.

    These three points need to be followed IN THAT ORDER! Many people have this order all messed up. If you want to find true happiness and joy in life, you must always focus on your faith and family before your job.

D = **D**ecisive:

1. Take responsibility. Your actions and your decisions always reveal who you really are. Take responsibility for your actions.

2. Make decisions. Some will be good, some great and some will be missteps but you must make decisions to move forward. Don't spend a lot of time vacillating over decisions.

3. Take action. I know, I keep bringing up action, but it's necessary to moving forward.

G = **G**et (up and go):

1. Work hard. Success is not a gift that is given. You must earn success, value, and respect.

2. Planes use all of their energy to take off but they cruise at 75% of power. Once you have succeeded in a challenge you may feel it is ok to back off some and still maintain. You have to know how much energy you need to keep flying.

3. Focus on what is next. Where will you go from where you are?

U = **U**nique:

1. Talent. Discover what you do best and what you love to do. Do not copy anybody else, be YOU!!

2. Fit into the organization you join. Each is different and is run differently. Pay attention to people and their interactions. If you can't

move forward, find a way to fit in and look for opportunities.

3. Be unique within the organization. Do not be afraid to take risks and challenges, that is how you grow in work and in life.

T = **T**enacity:

1. Yes, it's another repeat word, but put energy into your goals each and every day.

2. Keep on keeping on, it is easy to get distracted instead of moving forward.

3. Keep your eye on the goal. Don't take your eye off that target.

S = **S**atisfied:

1. Be grateful for what you have and what God puts in your path. It is much more satisfying when you are happy with the abundance, adventure and the love in your life. You are like no one else, be happy about it!

2. Enjoy what you do in life. Don't take a job just for money. Focus on what YOU LOVE!

3. Thank God each and every day for the blessings you have. It is essential to be grateful.

"Well, there you go, **BOLD GUTS**. I don't think there is any better focus to help you achieve your dreams." The professor finished with a smile.

"That is simply cool" Lynn sighed as she looked up from her phone.

DADS GIFT TO ME

"Ok, but wait just a minute" Tom said, looking up from his phone, "the last part of your sentence is 'dads gift to me". Are you saying that all of this joy, focus and success comes from our dads?"

"Yeah" I chimed in. "That part of the sentence surprised me too. We have gone along with this so far, but how is it all given to us from our dads?"

"Well, in case you haven't figured it out by now, the words mean something entirely different when we lay out the acronym. And you are certainly correct, nothing important is really given to you by anybody else. You must earn it," the Professor responded.

"Ok then," Lynn said "what does the rest of the sentence mean?"

"Glad you asked. Here we go, **DADS GIFT TO ME**. Let's start with the acronym, then go a little deeper.

DAD = **D**emand for what you do! **A**bility to do it! **D**ifficulty to replace you! All of this = Success.

The Demand for what you do is necessary to develop your skills. A good friend of mine used to say you should periodically get a 'checkup from the neck up'. If we are all people in basically good physical health, the value we bring to any company and to ourselves comes from our knowledge. Your education is never over because the world is always changing, so your ability and knowledge needs to change as well. Your skill set needs to be geared to the demand for it."

"So, we need to research the job market?" mused Tom.

"Of course, but it is not only about knowledge. It is about your Ability to use that knowledge. In business, there are always people with skills ranging from mediocre to excellent, with the majority being just average. The higher you are on the skill curve, the more valuable you are, and it becomes more Difficult to replace you. Just remember, all of your value is not compensated by money. You should be learning as well as earning and growing, so you need to find that balance. I think you'll agree that all of this together will equal Success." he said, smiling.

We all looked at each other and nodded in agreement.

"**GIFT** = **G**ood **I**ntention **F**or **T**oday. When we get up each morning, our intention should be to focus on doing good for others. It helps if you start each day spending time talking to God to let him know what is on your mind, both good and bad. Good and bad ebb and flow throughout our lives. Be thankful for the good and try to understand how to handle the challenges. That is what life is all about, and that is what **TO ME** in the sentence means. In other words, giving to others:

TO ME = **T**o **O**thers - **M**eans **E**verything!!
Helping others is what makes life worthwhile. Regardless of your skill, abundance or challenges, always help others."

"Wow that's a lot to think about, Professor, really deep!" Tom commented.

"Well thank you, I believe it is great foundation for being a winner in life." He stated.

"No Acronym?" I teased.

"Well, we could make one, if you want to? Let's see, a **WINNER** is the **W**illingness to learn. **I**ntegrity is doing what is right even if it hurts in the short term. **N**ever, compromise the integrity you establish. I repeated that, because it is that important" he said smiling. "And once lost, you will not get it back. **N**ow, don't wait or procrastinate. Take action so you can move forward. **E**nthusiastically approach work, life, and your passion. Enthusiasm shows and it is contagious. **R**emember where you came from. Where you are going is a result of challenges you have overcome and what you have learned along the way. After reaching the heights, stay very humble." He concluded.

"Professor, you are unbelievable, and so much fun to talk with, I have to get going though." Lynn said.

We began to get up to leave.

"Yes, I have to get someplace myself," he said "but one last thought I want you to leave with."

"Remember to look up at the sky and the adversity and strife will disappear in the blink of an eye. The kid's song tells us that "Life is but a dream." The older you get the faster time will go, or so it will seem. You need to make each day count toward YOUR fantastic scheme to make life as grand as you can. They say time runs away so slowly, yet walks away so fast. You cannot build your future if you are living in your past. Stay focused on what's ahead of you, and keep your vision great and grand. When your memories are greater than your dreams, life gets very difficult indeed. So, set your goals and believe in yourself as you go rowing down life's stream. Be brave and bold enough to make your dreams the biggest you can imagine!" he concluded with a smile.

Our heads were buzzing as we headed down the stairs.

CHAPTER 4

Motivating Factors

When we went back to the office a couple of weeks later, the outer office was empty, but the light was on, so we went back to see the Professor. As usual he seemed glad to see us.

I could hardly wait to get started. "I was telling Lynn and Tom, that you had mentioned a different way of looking at success."

He quickly jumped in, "I don't know if different is the proper word but the correct, way of looking at success".

"Really Professor? That seems pretty bold!" Lynn was her usual direct self. "What makes you sure your definition is correct?" Tom and I both nodded.

The Professor smiled and replied, "Because, people should define their own success, and the problem is, most people let others define success for them."

"Not everyone does!" I replied. "I certainly don't let people define my success."

"Never?" His eyebrow raised when he spoke.

"Have you ever compared yourself to others? Or coveted something someone else had? Or look on Face Book or Snap Chat or Twitter and wish that was you? Do any of you do that?"

That made us stop and think.

"Too many people compare themselves to others because they are afraid to take the steps to reach their own goals." He continued.

"The more you allow fear to cloud your thinking the more of a habit it becomes. People who give over their minds to fear, any sort of fear, fail to direct their minds forward and begin to drift. Eventually they can drift into a whirlpool of hypnotic rhythm from which they may never escape."

"The mind acts upon one's dominating, or primary desires. This is not opinion, it is a fact. So be careful what you wish for, because your subconscious will work to achieve it."

"If you keep your mind focused on positive motivating factors, you will move toward your goals. There are seven motivating factors that will help you get there."

"Well, that sounds interesting!" I said "What in the world would those be?"

"Ok, but you'll want to take notes on this. The first is Love. It is what everybody wants and desires, from family, of course, but people also want to find someone to love and spend their adult life with. Whether it is concerts, shows, hiking or books, you need to share with someone. Love is critical for long term joy and success, not necessarily marriage, but certainly a close relationship through family or friends is important."

"The second is sex," he began.

"Are you kidding me Professor? You are going to talk about that?" Tom sputtered, starting to turn red.

"Well, you are all adults and certainly aware of it in this society, so yes, we need to discuss it. Keep in mind that if we are talking about emotions that God gave us, that emotion is certainly one of them. We try to find our soul mate; someone to meet our physical and emotional needs. The search for someone to bring pleasure along with challenges is definitely something that motivates us."

"Third, there is material wealth. We all desire money and position or at least the perception of it. This has driven people throughout history and in every generation."

"Hold it, Professor," Lynn popped in, "What do you mean by 'perception' of wealth?"

"Wealth is not constant. Different generations view it and react to it differently. Our money used to be backed by gold rather than just being a promissory paper. Before credit cards became popular, people were often allowed to charge groceries and other supplies, to the provider. Credit cards made it easier to enjoy now and pay later. They also allow us to appear more successful because we can have more goods without waiting until we can afford them. At the same time, inflation is decreasing the value of the money we do have. It's a no-win situation when the interest on our credit cards actually decreases the money you have to spend. Many go into deep debt just to APPEAR wealthy. If you get into that routine, it is very hard to get out of it."

"I can see how that could happen." Tom mused.

"Here's another bit of advice on money. Eventually, you will probably buy a house, and need a loan. As you pay back the mortgage, you will be paying off most of the interest first. The key is to put another check for $50.00 or $100.00 with each payment with the notation 'Apply to Principal'. This can literally cut your 30-year mortgage in half to 15 years and save you tens of thousands of dollars on the loan. When money is tight you may only put down an extra $20 or $30, but DO IT!" He stopped to be sure we were paying attention.

"The interesting thing about these three motivations is that they are the focus of about 95% of everyone's efforts. It's simply the way we are and it's encouraged by the prosperous and open environment we enjoy in the United States."

"The fourth motivator is Self-Preservation. Of course, we all want to survive, be positive, and make a difference in people's lives. Most of us don't spend a lot of time focusing on it, but self-preservation will take precedence over almost everything when it is threatened."

"We just saw that during the hurricanes," I said.

"Very true," the Professor agreed. "And, closely linked with our self-preservation is number five, our desire for Freedom, both of the Body and Mind. We are especially blessed to have that freedom in this country. In your life, you will be exposed to activities and fads that are not good for either your body or your mind. You will see people sitting around watching tv and eating fast food and other things that do nothing for the mind or the body's health. Now is the time to form good habits. Stay active physically and mentally. It will help you explore all the other things that life can offer." The Professor was looking very pleased as he finished.

"Wow, that's a lot to think about" I said "I can see where it would be harder to change when you get older."

"Yes, indeed" the Professor nodded in agreement. "And it is critical to keep your mind active and growing. Remember, your education is not done when you graduate. If it is, you will soon be left behind. If you keep learning, you will be able to analyze situations, verbalize your observations and make optimal choices."

"You need to observe closely, understand what you are seeing, and act on your understanding. Decisive action makes all the difference," he concluded.

"Professor, this is all so deep it makes my head spin, but I love it!" Lynn jumped in. We had to agree. There would be a lot of conversations between us during the next week.

"While you are learning, let's talk about the sixth motivator, personal recognition. We are willing to give 100% for something we believe in, and if we get the recognition we deserve, we will find a way to give even more. It's hard to sustain an effort if you don't get credit for your hard work, and even worse if someone else takes credit for it. Remember what that feels like when you are in charge, so you can recognize the effort others put into the project," he finished.

"That makes a lot of sense," Tom said, "but you said there were seven motivating factors?"

"You are correct, Tom. The seventh motivator is one that makes a lot of people uncomfortable, but it is my favorite. It is our desire for perpetuation - a place in eternity. We want to know that after this life is done, we will continue to exist. Our faith and our belief in eternal life affect all our thoughts and actions. If you truly feel blessed, how can you not try to be a blessing to others?"

"Stay focused on your faith and your path will stay ethical, you'll sleep better at night and your attitude will be more positive. Once you achieve some success, you will encounter the hardest part of all: be humble. It will be easy for your ego to get out of whack and for you to start believing that all that success is self-generated. If you combine the skills you have been given with the sweat of your brow, you will see the signs of the creator throughout your life."

"I have been fortunate to have lived for quite some time, and here is what has worked for me. Be thankful every day for the blessings you have already received, and know that you have an angel watching over you. Be open to the possibilities and God will show you the signs. At this age I've learned not to look outside myself for fulfillment. Faith, trust, values and service are not things that can be bought nor can positive thinking."

"Wow, that's a lot to think about, and I guess I agree, but you're right, we don't think about those things every day. I can see the benefit of staying positive, but are there ever negative motivators that hold us back?" Tom asked.

"Yes, of course, but there are really only two. The first is easy to discuss, but the second covers a lot of steps. We might have to continue it another time, because I know it's close to your class time."

"Oh, that's ok. We can skip class." I volunteered.

"You most certainly cannot skip class" said the Professor, narrowing his eyes as he held my gaze, "and Lynn cannot be late for work. Haven't you been paying attention?"

"Relax Professor, we're not cutting work or classes" Lynn said, calmly. "But I would like to hear about those negative motivators."

"All right" said the Professor taking a deep breath. The number one negative motivator is Revenge. When things don't go or turn out the way people want, they want to blame someone, and then get revenge. Revenge is especially negative because it wastes so much of your time on negative attitudes and actions. All actions are like boomerangs: what you give out will come back to you - it's the way things work. Think about it, have you ever truly felt better after you have been involved in an incident of revenge?"

That had us all thinking.

"As we close today, I want you to remember this recipe for happiness and a good life: Believe in yourself and in your abilities. When you dream, dream big and believe in your vision. Keep your mind focused on your values and principals, knowing that you are truly one of God's children and part of His beautiful plan."

"Professor, you are the best! Thank you for your guidance. You're right, this is going to take a while to soak up. We'll be back to see you soon." As we left, I looked back at the Professor, and from the way he was smiling, he knew he had gotten through to us."

CHAPTER 5

Function Factor

It had been two weeks since our last meeting with the Professor. Lynn, Tom and I had talked often about that lesson. There was so much we still hadn't figured out, but the Professor was changing the way we looked at everything. Part of it was his easy way of making it all seem so logical without putting pressure on us.

We decided to swing by before classes this morning for a quick visit. We met in the lobby and hurried up to the office. The Professor seemed to be expecting us. Was he always in his office?

"Well hello you three, I thought I might be seeing you again soon!" the Professor said. He hadn't even turned around to see who was there.

"Hi Professor!" we said in unison.

"Is it ok to chat with you a little this morning, Professor?" I asked.

"Certainly, anytime is good with me, I am here to help you learn. How have you all been?"

"We are still digesting your last lesson. It really made us think. It was very deep, Professor!" Lynn said.

"Well, that is the point of all this. Learning goes on all the time if we are open to it. Have you been open to it?" He asked with a knowing smile.

"Ok Professor, you certainly got us interested in finding our own happiness. We may not always get what we want, but we can sure make the most of what we get during our search. Last time, we were just getting into how things function in the world of work. I'm still putting it all together." Tom said shaking his head.

"Well, I certainly have thoughts on most things in life at my age. So, would you like to hear some of them about career selection?" The Professor paused and looked at us.

He had our full attention.

"Let's start with a math class," the Professor began.

"Really? I'm not very good at math." Lynn said skeptically.

"One of my philosophies in math is $EQ + V = AB2$, which stands for the **E**motional **Q**uotient + **V**ision = **A**ttitude and **B**elief to the second power."

"Acronyms again?" I asked.

"Well sort of, you see, we often complicate things in life. These are some simple but effective ways to approach the challenges you will face. Your success, as always, depends on your attitude and your approach. Start with your vision. You need to know where you are going, then approach that vision with a great attitude. Your belief in achieving your vision is so important it is squared." The Professor was on a roll.

"Understand that each job is a learning experience. If you are paying attention, you will gain experience and knowledge in every job, but first you must get the job. My formula for getting the job is this: start with **TWO + 2** then **SOAR**." He waited for our response.

"Oh, that makes it perfectly clear, doesn't it?" Lynn said, looking totally confused.

"It does, if you'll stay with me on this. In an interview when you are asked questions, just apply the **TWO**, always **T**alk **W**ith **O**ptimism! People do not want to hear negatives, so regardless of the question, answer realistically, but with optimism. Another thing you hear is 'tell me a little about yourself'. That is where the **2**-minute drill comes in. Practice your two-minute response to that request. Tell them about your life, your experience, your passion, and your successes along with what you have learned. Here is why you must practice: you must be able to speak about yourself and your background for about **2** minutes with no hesitation, no pauses, no 'ums' or ahs' while looking the interviewer in the eye. It's not easy unless you practice it, but it is very impressive in an interview."

"Another interview part is often 'tell me about a challenge you faced in the past and how you handled it'. This is where **SOAR** comes in. In most interviews, we either talk too much or not enough. Either way, it makes you look unprepared. When you practice for your interview, start with the **S**ituation you faced, then explain the **O**bstacles you faced. Move forward with the **A**ctions you took and the **R**esults you achieved. Then stop! Be quiet and wait for the next question. Prepare for at least two different experiences, since they may ask for another example. Those two-minute drills will work in your favor every time. My students who have practiced this usually leave the interview with a job offer." He paused again to see if we were still following him.

"This is stuff they never taught us when we were learning to create resumes, but I can certainly see how it would work." Tom said.

The Professor nodded and continued. "The best way to get where you are going is to use a **MAP**. By that, I mean a **M**anagement **A**pplication **P**rincipal."

This sounded important, so we all began taking notes again.

"Let's start with the **PIE** MAP. Once you get your job you can use this constantly. You should **P**lan, **I**mplement and **E**valuate everything. Your **P**lan will give the direction or approach, so you can **I**mplement the steps in the order you have mapped out. As you begin to see progress, it will be tempting to jump ahead and possibly skip some steps – don't. Since you are part of a team, you will need to **E**valuate your progress by checking with the members of your team to ensure that all parts of the plan are completed properly. Too often, this is the end of the process, because people forget to follow up and to revise the plan to fit changing situations."

Tom looked up. "So how do you evaluate things when a whole team is involved?"

"Evaluation is easy using the **WWW** map, which stands for **W**ho does **W**hat by **W**hen? You work on projects as a team, so it's essential to know **W**ho does **W**hat by **W**hen. This keeps the team from wasting valuable time on duplication of effort. It is easy to see who deserves credit for completing and contributing (an entirely different topic of motivation). Everyone knows exactly what is expected of them and the timeline involved, and they will also know exactly what value each person brings to the team."

"Professor, I know this will help in our careers, but I think it could help on school projects, too." I said.

"You will find these principles can be adapted to many situations," the Professor agreed.

"Well" Lynn jumped in "I see this every day at the company where I work and I know it could help me become more valuable to them."

"Lynn, it is funny you should say that, since that's my next point. To determine your value to an organization, you should evaluate yourself using the **SSC** MAP."

"Ok, I'm ready, what is the **SSC** MAP, Professor?" Tom prodded.

"A great question, Tom, I knew you would ask. It is how your supervisors look at your performance and determine how you advance in your career. It also works in every aspect of your life. The first **S** is **S**tart. Analyze what you need to **S**tart doing to increase your value to the organization. Career paths rarely run perfectly smooth since other people with different goals are also involved. Because of this you will develop talents and skills you never knew you had. Always look for opportunities and be willing to do what is necessary to improve yourself and the organization."

"The other **S** is the flip side of the coin. What should you **S**top doing? As you develop confidence, you sometimes bite off more than you can chew. At these times, you may notice that some of your thoughts and actions do not deliver good results. You need to stop those thoughts and actions. Be honest with yourself so you can focus on what you do best and put your energy there."

"That brings up the **C**. What should you **C**ontinue to do? You were hired for your position based on the potential your employers saw in you. Don't lose sight of that. If you practice these three points, you can't help but grow in the organization and as a positive person." He concluded.

"I see," Tom said. "It's back to the **P**lan, **I**mplement and **E**valuate MAP!"

"That's right. All these principles overlap and they work well together."

"It's all starting to fit." I said. "I can see how having these MAP's could be important to our careers."

"If you follow them, you can't go wrong," the professor leaned back smiling.

"Professor, are you implying if we apply these things we can never go wrong?" Lynn jumped in.

"Never is a pretty strong word, Lynn, because things are always changing, but it certainly increases the odds of a favorable outcome. Remember that your mindset and your attitude still determine your reaction to any situation. When you add emotion to any situation, it acts like a magnet and you tend to attract more of the same to you. This is why you want to stay positive, because the attraction works just as well on negative thoughts. Your mind will work to deliver what you think about – ALWAYS!"

"Often you see two people with the same upbringing and opportunities, but one is very successful and the other is not. The difference usually comes down to their outlook and their attitudes. Outlook helps establish your habits, and habits establish your dominant thoughts, which attract things that are similar, so stay positive."

"Does that mean I'll attract more money?" Tom said grinning.

"I know you are joking, Tom, but there is a universal law of compensation, which some call karma. You will eventually reap what you sow. Does this mean that good guys always win and bad guys always lose? Not necessarily in the short term, but it usually evens out in the end. Making the best choices is easier if you don't lose focus on your faith and your core values as you move through your career."

"Too often, people don't think about this until they are overwhelmed. At which time they say 'Oh God, please help me and I promise to be more faithful'. When things get better, they forget their promise and revert back to their old ways until they are overwhelmed again. It is much better to live in harmony with your faith. The Bible, in John 6:29 states 'This is the work of God, that you believe in the one He sent.' I know this may make you uncomfortable, but I'm telling you that it works. Believing is not just for times of crisis. Every day, God presents us with numerous opportunities to apply our faith and thereby build our character."

"So, faith can keep you from feeling like a failure when things don't work out?" I asked.

"Failure is a man-made circumstance. It is never real until it has been accepted as such, otherwise it is just a setback in the journey to your goal. Since failure is a state of mind, it is something you can control if you decide to. Nature does not force people to fail. God does not want you to fail. He wants you to learn from your growth and challenges alike."

"I've noticed that faith is a recurring theme for you, Professor, but does it really come up that much in everyday life?" Tom asked.

"Actually, it is interesting just how often it does come up if we pay attention. Just yesterday I met a woman at the flea market who was selling homemade cookies. She was considerably older than the other vendors, so I inquired about her health. She said she was doing just fine and as we talked, I could almost sense an aura around her. When I asked if she was always in this good a mood, she told me she was, because she knew a secret. I asked if she would share it. She said that attitude was the greatest gift of all, because you could use it to make the best of every day. She said she was truly blessed to have me enter her life at this time. I told her that if a blessing was there, it surely had to be mine. Then she left me with this:"

"Please understand that whether we are young or old, we are all part of the big dance. You see, God is playing the music as we glide across the floor, and you may find a blessing far away or right next door. Please be kind to any and all of those you meet in this pathway we call life. For you need to understand God is watching all we do and He will teach you to dance just right!"

"So, there you go. Faith is simply the best way to dance through life," the Professor said.

"Professor you never cease to amaze us. I hope you know the effect you are having on all of us." I said.

"You got that right!" Lynn exclaimed.

"Totally agree. This is crazy good stuff, Professor!"

"Well, that is what Professors are for. I am so glad you've been paying attention. Now you just need to remember what you learned so you can implement it. We'll talk again soon, but right now you need to get to class."

As we got up, I spontaneously gave the Professor a quick hug. To my surprise, both Lynn and Tom followed my lead. We were really getting attached to the Professor.

CHAPTER 6

Depends on How You Look at Things

It was a Monday afternoon in January and we were sitting at Troy's Diner catching up after the holidays. None of us had seen the Professor for over a month. It's not that we planned it, but between classes, the swim team and jobs, we didn't seem to have any spare time.

"I can't believe it's been so long since we've seen him" Lynn said.

"I was sure I'd run into him on campus, but I haven't. Have you, Tom?" I asked.

"Nope, I haven't seen him either, which is surprising, 'cause the campus isn't that big. Of course, we could drop in on him, we have a standing invitation, don't we? Besides, I don't have class till 3:00." Tom hinted.

"Sounds good to me. I don't work till this evening." Lynn volunteered.

"I'm in!" I said. "I'm sure he wonders what happened to us, and I wonder what else he has to teach us."

We finished lunch and headed to the Professor's office. We quickly reviewed some of the past lessons on the way. Each of us had found ways to put parts of them into practice.

When we knocked on the door, we were surprised to hear the Professor call out "Come in, come in, I've been expecting you." I'm not sure how that could be, but he really seemed like he had been waiting for us.

"It has been a while since I have seen you three, I certainly hope you all had a great holiday season and enjoyed your time off. I hope you got a little time off work." He said to Lynn.

"I spent a couple of weeks with my family." She responded. "Christmas has always been an important holiday for us."

"It should be for everyone, although the new trend is not to call it Christmas!" He said, shaking his head "Some people simply do not understand what faith is."

Tom smiled. "There's that faith again. I guess that's why we're here. We've got faith that you have something more to teach us."

"That is an interesting thing to say. Can I assume that you have time for a little lesson today?" He asked, looking at each of us in turn.

"So what is the topic for today?" I asked.

"Well, since Tom dropped the F-bomb maybe we should talk about that!" He smiled at our wide-eyed shocked expressions.

"That can't mean what we think it does!" Lynn said.

The professor laughed a little. "Certainly not the version that I hear around the campus by the more immature young adults. Let's start with an acronym for **FUN FAN.**"

"You have an acronym for fun fan? Why am I not surprised?" I said. This was one class I was glad to be back in.

"Yes, I do. **FUN FAN** is **F**ocus **U**nderstanding **N**eeds-**F**ully **A**ppreciating **N**ow!" He was looking very smug.

"Holy smokes Professor! You have acronyms for everything!" Tom exclaimed

"No, not everything, but it is a great way to start dropping the **F** bomb theory. Whatever you do in life you need to **F**ocus on what is going on around you both in the work world and your personal world. Each of us is unique and we all have different dreams, aspirations, and challenges. We are all threads in the tapestry of the universe. Notice I did not say 'special'. Please drop that silly self-description from your vocabulary. Once you **U**nderstand that, you can try to understand the **N**eeds of others. **F**ully **A**ppreciate **N**ow means you enjoy the moment regardless of who you are with or what you are doing. Time never goes backwards, so focus on getting the best out of every moment."

"Now let's talk about **FTD**." He began.

"Like the flower shop?" I asked.

"I know that is the way most people think of **FTD,** but I look it as one of the major pitfalls of people's careers. It means **F**ailing **T**o **D**eliver." He said

"Failing to deliver what?" Lynn asked

"Results," the Professor said, "or at least excellent results. Failing to deliver excellent results."

"And is that a problem?" I asked.

"Remember this sentence when you work your way up to management. You will need it for evaluating, coaching, and creating a winning team. it helps you to understand how everyone is approaching their obligations. **FTD** please **S**end **S**ome to **E**very **H**ome."

"FTD - Send Some to Every Home?" Lynn repeated, a little dismayed. "That is just bizarre. What on earth does that even mean?"

"It is just a simple way to remember the first letters of the words. I guess you could say **FTD-SSEH**, but you know how I like acronyms. If someone on your team is **FTD,** or **F**ailing **T**o **D**eliver, they usually have one of these four problems."

"**S**end **S**ome to **E**very **H**ome- **S** is Lack of **S**chooling. They don't have the knowledge to do their job. This could be a lack of training or lack of coaching. If they are given the training, but still cannot perform their job, maybe they are not capable. A good leader will notice this and make decisions to preserve their team. Teams, like chains are only as strong as their weakest link. This does not mean that you cannot help other team members, but it should not interfere with your own responsibilities."

"The second **S** is Lack of **S**kill that they need for that job. They may simply not have the skill set their job requires. In this case, either they are trying to fit a square peg into a round hole of the need so to speak maybe they can be reassigned and remain a productive part of the team, but that doesn't always work either. They may need to be replaced on the team. In the early part of your careers you will probably observe this, so keep these FTD's in mind when you are running a team."

"Failing to deliver on the **E** is the lack of **E**ffort. Some people simply don't put in the effort to get their job done. If they have the training and skill, the leader has to get them to work harder or add incentives to boost productivity. This may involve counseling and clearly explaining what is expected of them, but if they are just lazy, they may need to be replaced. A rotten apple will spoil the whole basket if it is allowed to stay, and team members notice quickly when someone is getting a free ride."

"The **H** stands for the lack of **H**onesty. When someone on the team lacks integrity, the whole team is labeled untrustworthy. You simply cannot work in this environment, and others will not work with you. If your team cannot be trusted, your own integrity suffers, and anything the team accomplishes is diminished."

"Of course, you want the team to accomplish things you can be proud of, but don't be arrogant. James 6:4 reminds us 'God resists the proud, but grants grace to the humble'. As you work on building a solid team remember these rules – they always apply."

"That sounds like good advice to me." Tom said. "But what was all that about the **F**-bombs?"

The professor chuckled. "Ok, let's start with the 3 F's that show how to handle upset people. We all have to do that sometimes, don't we? For example, CC, aren't you captain of the swim team?"

I was puzzled, because I didn't remember ever telling him that, but nodded in agreement.

"And Lynn, you are in sales. Are people ever upset there?"

Lynn rolled her eyes dramatically.

"Tom, you work in the service industry. Do you ever deal with upset people?"

Tom nodded, remembering some of his more difficult customers.

"So, everyone deals with unhappy people at times. Here is a way to deal with that. The three **F**'s stand for **F**eel – **F**elt – **F**ound. When you deal with someone who is upset and wants someone to hear their complaint, listen. Let them tell you how they **F**eel. Look at them and let them know you understand how they **F**eel because you have experienced something similar and **F**elt that way too. Then explain how others handled it positively and what they **F**ound. It's a quick and easy process that you will find many uses for."

"Does it always work?" Tom asked.

"Nothing works all the time, but the more problem-solving tools you have, the better." The Professor advised.

I knew a couple of situations I could try that in right away.

"This is good info," I said, "But I still feel a little weird about calling them **F**-bombs. You hinted that there were more?"

"Let me start with a question. Have you ever met someone who you just know has a relationship with the Lord? I'm not talking about someone who brags about how religious they are or who quotes scripture constantly. They just seem to live out Psalms 34:2 - 'I will bless the Lord at all times". It is evident in the way they speak and the way they live their lives. They make it a habit to honor the Lord in everything they do. I hope a similar attitude blossoms in you as you grow. If you have true **F**aith, you will find needed strength in difficult times."

"You should always have **F**aith in God. Recognize your blessings in good times and you will have somewhere to turn in difficult times. Have **F**aith in other people. It has been said that everyone is doing the best they can with who they are and what they know at any given time. Your faith in others will be rewarded more than it will be disappointed. Have Faith in yourself. This is a very important one. When we stumble, misstep, or fall, we need to remain positive, pick ourselves up and move on. Have Faith in life. God has placed you on this earth for a purpose, so live the best life you can and enjoy your time here."

When the Professor looked at me I'm sure he saw the tears forming in my eyes. I could tell the others were deeply moved too. We all were raised with Faith, but when we got busy, we didn't think about it that much.

"Wow," I said. "That kind of wraps it all up, doesn't it?"

"Almost, but not quite" the Professor cautioned. The next three F's should be put in the following order, they are your life's priorities. Put Faith first in life. It is the framework which supports everything else. Next has to be your Family. Your family is your support system. Please note that your 'family' does not always have to be blood relatives, but you will need someone to share your joys and to uplift you in tough times. Don't forget to do your part and be supportive of the members of your own family" He said.

"I know how scary it is when my dad has heart problems. Our family really relies on each other for support." I said.

"Lynn, I know your dad had cancer, and my grandpa has developed Alzheimer's which is stressful for him and all the rest of us." Tom said quietly.

The Professor nodded "You can see what I mean, but one big problem is when we put the third **F – F**inance out of order. If you put finances first you lose the true value of your life. When you have a secure faith and family, finance adds to the fullness of your life, but is not the main goal. It's funny, but if you establish your faith and have your family, the finances often occur as a part of your life."

"I get that, Professor, but what do you do when people distract you from your goals? It seems to happen a lot lately." Lynn asked.

"The quick solution is photography! The Professor quipped.

"What?" Lynn sputtered.

"You need to look at life like a *camera*! You need to *focus* on what is important to you. You then *develop* your skills and *views* from how you handle the *negative* things that happen to create a *positive* outcome. You can learn to *capture* the good times, *roll* with the punches, and know that you can always take another *shot*."

"But seriously, I understand that people are a challenge. Remember, your faith tells you that God is always on your side, and that is more than enough to balance any scale. Your support system is always with you **if you believe in Him**."

"That said I understand people challenge us always as a matter of fact, experts tell us that for every negative comment we hear it takes five positive comments to balance that out. Therefore, it is much easier to get discouraged than to feel encouraged as we go along, remember though God is always on your side. He is always at work offering you his encouragement if you are listening. Now does that mean you are not going to be challenged or fail once and awhile? Of course not, but remember he is always there to support you and help you learn **if you believe in Him.**"

"Do you remember when you were a little child? A child's whole world is based on belief. They believed someone will feed them, protect them and love them. They believed what they are told, at least until it is proven false. And what is it with a kid and a Band-Aid. It seems to be the best miracle cure ever conceived for scrapes, bumps, and bruises or anything that hurts. That Band-Aid will fix it because they believe. This plastic strip, believe it or not, spews magic from its very pores. If you are not convinced, watch it work when a small kid takes a fall and see how that Band-Aid stops the pain and tears. It works the same for adults. Your dreams stand little chance of coming true unless you believe in them. In case you need a reminder," he said, handing each of them a Band-Aid, "keep this with you to remind you of the importance of believing. Believe in yourself, in your dreams, in your family and most of all, in the Lord's love and guidance."

"Professor, it's amazing how fast the time goes when we're around you." Tom said, staring at the Band-Aid in his hand. "You make it easy to believe in ourselves."

I agreed. "Today's lesson was off the charts! Thank you."

"I'll certainly have a different perspective when I hear the term 'F-bomb' next time" Lynn said, grinning.

"You are all so very welcome and I look forward to seeing you all again soon, but remember, if you don't use the lesson, it won't be of much value," the Professor concluded.

We all agreed as we gathered our books and headed for class.

CHAPTER 7

Building with Consistency

Graduation was rapidly approaching, and there were lots of activities for seniors, so it was two weeks later when I joined Tom and Lynn for lunch before we visited the Professor. We went to the School of Business and, as usual, the Professor's office light was on. We could hear him moving around inside, but when we opened the door, he wasn't there. Then we saw him coming down the spiral staircase from the landing where the recliner sat.

"Were you up there taking a nap?" Tom asked.

"Not today, although I do that from time to time, I was reading." he replied.

He sat at the desk and motioned us all to sit down.

"How are you three today?" He asked.

"We wanted to catch up since we hadn't seen you in a while" Lynn said.

"Yeah Professor." Tom added. "We thought we'd see you around campus. Have you been subbing?"

"Yes, I have. I've noticed you across the quad from time to time, but you were too far away to say hello. Is anything exciting happening in your lives?"

"Not unless you count the way we view nearly everything, like who we are, how we grow, and what we want to accomplish in life! I'm surprised you don't have an acronym for that." Tom said smiling.

"Well it's not really an acronym. It's more an observation on your self-talk. Your self-talk should be directed to the person you are trying to become, so every morning you should tell yourself things like this:

I am an honest, intelligent, organized, responsible, committed, teachable person. I am sober and loyal. I am a self-employed person regardless of who signs my pay check. I am optimistic, punctual, enthusiastic, goal oriented, and a smart worker."

"If you start your day this way, you will be ready to face anything the world throws at you. It also helps to start the day thankful for your spiritual foundation, your life, your health, your job, and those around you."

"To be a self-starter, who is disciplined, focused, dependable, and energetic, you must remain positive. Being a team player means being aware how your actions affect others, but not sacrificing your own integrity. And, being aware lets you see opportunities as they arise." When the Professor stopped for a breath, Lynn jumped in.

"I knew this was going to get deep today!" she said.

"Oh, there's nothing deep or even mysterious about it. It's a slow steady process, but mostly it's common sense, which maybe isn't that common today. Just realize that we are all on a non-stop journey and it includes every experience we have and what we make of it."

"Think of it this way: when you retire, what would you like the speaker to say about you at your retirement dinner, or when you eventually leave this earth what do you want your eulogy to include? If you consider each day as a building block in your life, what will the house you build look like?"

They all looked at each other shrugging their shoulders wondering where he was headed.

"Let's say you work 40 years in your career, that is approximately 10,000 days, or blocks. Early in your career it is hard to get started, but it is important to get a solid foundation as soon as possible. Not every block will be suitable for building, the way some people spend their spare time" he smiled nodding and continued. "So, you must be willing to discard or modify some blocks. The way you assemble them determines what type of 'life house' you will build. It's not just the size of your house, but how it affects those in and around it. Your guiding principles are the skeleton or frame on which you will build as you go along in life."

"Wow" said Tom. "That's a lot to take in. We just went from self-talk to building blocks to bones!"

"Speaking of bones" the Professor continued, "as you go through life, you will encounter four types of bones. Some people are Wish Bones. They are dreamers who just wish 'someone' would do the things that need to be done. For exercise, they sidestep leadership roles and therefore dodge responsibility. Their life house is probably mid-sized with some nice rooms, but it is well below their capabilities."

"You will also meet Jaw Bones. They are busy analyzing and verbalizing, and are never short on opinions. Although they talk a lot about what they are going to do, they never do much actual work. Their main exercise is jumping to conclusions and pushing their luck." The Professor looked up to see that we were all grinning at his classification of people. "I take it you have already met a few of these types."

We all nodded.

"Then you may also have met some Knuckle Bones. They always knock what others are doing. It seems that nobody can do things right but them, and yet they don't do much that is positive. They get their exercise by running down the people and ideas around them. It is hard to be around people like this, so they are often left behind or move on. It is fitting that their life house is a travel trailer, since they are not a permanent or positive influence on those around them."

"Then the last group are the Backbones. These are the people who GET THINGS DONE! They make the most of their skills and knowledge to construct wonderful life houses. When you spend time around them, you feel enriched. Their exercise is uplifting people, supporting others and working with ideas."

"I think we have all met people in each of these categories. Do these classifications really make life easier?" I asked.

"I think it may save you a lot of time if you realize the type of person you are working with, so you know what to expect from them as far as output. After all, life is like a backgammon game."

"Backgammon?" I blurted out. "My dad plays backgammon. How is backgammon like life?"

"The game is based on the 80/20 rule. It relies about 80% on your skill and 20% on your luck rolling the dice.

Life is like that because you have skills but you have to take chances to move forward. Remember, a turtle can't move forward unless it sticks its neck out!" He was truly enjoying this.

"Well I will certainly take any good luck, Professor, but how do we build our skills when our daily work is a rut that is hard to move out of?" Lynn asked, looking puzzled.

"A super great question!" The professor exclaimed.

"Think of your life and your career in terms of the 5 **W**'s. The w's stand for the following and the order is important: why, where, when, what, and who. Let me explain: **W**hy are you heading in this direction in your life and career? First, you define your governing values and your purpose in life."

"**W**here is this going to take you? This lets you see possible outcomes and helps you clarify your long-range goals. You may need to adjust your direction somewhat. Since each step builds on the others, it is important to have a solid foundation."

"**W**hen are you going to take these steps? Once you have defined your goals, you need a timeline. If you know what steps are next, you will be prepared to act when the opportunity arises. Your timeline may move based on circumstances, but it is essential to have it as a guide."

"**W**hat will you have to do? What daily tasks fit with your plan. Things seldom happen as quickly as we would like, and our plans and God's plan for us may not be on the same schedule. As we grow in faith and acquire skills, we will figure that out. When God presents an opportunity, we need to be ready to take advantage of it."

"Everything you do will determine **W**ho you are as a person. If you recall, I spent a lot of time discussing the importance of faith: faith in yourself, in your support group, in your abilities and in God. Here is the part many people seem to forget God loves you, not some future you but the present you. Anything you accomplish through faith is an added bonus in your life."

"What you do is based on who you are as a person. Who you are as a person is based on your actions and your actions are based on your thoughts. What you think is based on your experiences and influences in life and your reactions to them. To understand growth better think of Corinthians 3:5 'Our qualification comes from God'. Throughout all our growth and challenges, God is never done with us. He continues to make us stronger as long as we keep our faith and believe in him."

"One of the great joys in life is finding 'God-moments', those unexpected moments that make you think of God, or strengthen your faith. It may be people you meet, moments in nature, things you observe, or music.

Keep your senses open for the good in the world and in people and your faith will be strengthened. Your faith and the faith of those around you will, in turn, allow you to withstand any adversities you face. You may not see how the Spirit is influencing you as you grow, but take some time to admire God's handiwork, and you will see that you are a marvel!"

"You are far stronger, capable and flexible than you think. You have 'the strength for everything' in Christ, who strengthens you (Philippians 4:13)! If you pray for situations, not in self-confidence, but in God-confidence, you can let go of pretenses and schemes, so you can accomplish great works. I know I get a little wound up on this, but it is truly the most important thing I can teach you," the Professor continued.

"It used to make me uncomfortable to hear people talk about faith" Tom said, "but the way you explain it makes it a natural part of life and growth."

"Yeah," Lynn added. "I always thought of faith as something you had or didn't have, not something that could be learned."

I was seeing a completely different side of my friends, and I liked it, I saw the Professor smiling as he replied.

"Every day you must make difficult decisions. You will act on those decisions and may not find out the consequences of those actions for years to come. Maybe that is the way God wants it, so you will work hard and try to win. If your efforts fail this time, have the courage to try again. If you got all your wishes and always won, why would you ever dream or grow? When you have a difficult decision to make, look into your heart, trust in your faith, and you can never really lose."

"Professor, you have a great way of sharing your knowledge with us." I said. "I'm going to miss coming to see you after I graduate."

"I'll miss seeing you too, but if you learned some of life lessons I will always be there with you. I know the three of you will always be in my heart. Let's not get all emotional, because I'm sure we'll be in touch on some level throughout your lives." He said, grinning.

"You're the best!" Lynn said.

"We can all agree on that. You certainly have given us a lot to think about, Professor." Tom said as he stood.

It was hard not to be emotional as we each hugged the Professor and prepared to leave. "I'll stay in touch." I promised.

CHAPTER 8

Ice Cream Instruction

It was an unusually warm Sunday and the three of us were in the park catching up, when Tom suggested we go to the ice cream shop. Today's flavor was cinnamon, our favorite. While we were standing in line, Lynn brought up our 'acronym meeting' with the Professor (we had given each of the meetings a name, so we immediately knew what she was talking about).

"I've been thinking a lot about the acronym meetings," she said. It was so deep that it took me a long time to sort it all out, but I think if we actually tried to live that way, we would truly be successful."

"You're probably right," mused Tom. "The Professor is really brilliant and so focused, but that office of his blows me away every time we walk in it."

"Excuse me, I'm sorry to interrupt," said a female voice behind us.

We turned around and were surprised to see three nuns standing in the line.

They had on their 'nun dresses', as Tom called them, full habits with headpieces like nuns used to wear years ago. They were all medium height, and probably in their mid-fifties, but their most exceptional feature was their beautiful smiles. They were warm and pleasant.

"No problem," I said. "Were you in a hurry do you need to cut in front of us?'

"Oh no, not at all, but we overheard you three talking about the Professor and his marvelous office. It reminded us of a professor we met when we were in college here. He loved acronyms too. That experience totally changed our lives, but there's no way it could be the same person, could it?" She looked puzzled, then remembered her manners. "I'm sorry, I'm Sister Margaret, and this is Sister Mary and Sister Louise."

We all shook hands and introduced ourselves.

"Why couldn't it be the same professor?" Tom asked.

"Well, it was over 35 years ago and he appeared to be in his late sixties back then, but it certainly brought back some great memories," Sister Mary said.

By now we were at the window and the young girl asked for our order.

"Please, Sisters, you can go ahead, we're not in any hurry" Lynn offered.

"Oh, no" Sister Mary said shaking her head, "It just sounded like you were talking about someone we knew."

"No worries," Tom responded, then looked into the window and said, "please get the sisters what they want as well."

"You don't have to do that." Sister Louise tried to refuse, but Tom was insistent.

"Nonsense, I'm buying, but we'd would love to pick your brains about this professor of yours. It sure sounds like the same one we met, but he doesn't look 90. He looks like you described, late sixties."

"Yes, please join us," I added.

"Well that is very kind of you. What would you like to know?" Sister Margaret said, obviously flattered.

They got their cones and we went to the outdoor round table.

"So, what did your professor look like?" Lynn asked.

"Let's see, he was short, with a wild white mane of hair, he usually wore glasses, was very energetic, and always seemed to be smiling. If I had to describe him in one word I would call him Professor Positive." Sister Mary replied.

The three of us nodded in unison. "That has to be the same Professor" Tom said. "We were just talking about the acronym he taught us. 'I value luck success an action system with courage, bold guts, dads gift to me.' It really was life changing. Is that what he taught you?"

"No, that wasn't exactly what he taught us, it's interesting that he schooled all three of you at the same time too," Sister Louise commented. "He certainly did change our career directions," she said shaking her head.

"What were you three planning to do?" Lynn asked.

Sister Margaret answered first. "I was going into the landscaping business and possibly open a nursery down the road. I guess now you can say, I landscape people."

Sister Mary volunteered next. "I was going into sales. I've always been pretty persuasive and enjoy working with people. Now I guess I'm selling the Lord to everyone I meet."

Sister Louise leaned forward. "I always thought I was going to be in management. I was good with budgeting, tracking income, banking and accounting. Like my two sisters, I help manage people now, and it's all because of that one sentence."

I couldn't hold back "What in the world is the sentence that convinced you three to become nuns?"

They looked at each other and smiled, then Sister Margaret answered. "Here is what he told us 'Always remember this, no matter where life takes you, and never give up on it. **ALL FEAR** of **LIFE** is a **MAN FROG LIVING** a **BIBLE LIFE** of **FAITH**."

"What?" I stammered. "You're going to have to explain that one, Sister. Even though I'm a Catholic I don't get it. Would a Catholic acronym apply to everyone?"

"Let me ask you this," Sister Mary replied. "In the different Christian faiths do people believe that Jesus was born?"

We all nodded.

"In other Christian faiths do they believe Jesus was crucified and went to heaven?"

"Of course, they do" Lynn said.

"Do other Christian faiths believe that Jesus rose from the dead and came back to earth alive three days later?" Sister Louise continued.

"Isn't that what makes them Christians?" Tom asked.

"Yes, it is. So, we all believe the same regardless of what we call our Christian faith. I know there are different rituals and rules in churches but it's based on the same basic beliefs. One thing you may not know about the Catholic faith is that the Sunday morning scripture readings are the same in every Catholic church. They don't fluctuate based on anyone's decision of what reading to share. The priest's homily and interpretation may vary, but the readings are the same."

She had our attention. I could see she would have been great in sales.

Sister Mary continued. "If we all believe that Jesus was the son of God and he died for our sins we are all on the same path. John 3:16 – "That God so loved the world that he gave his one and only Son, that whoever believes in him shall not perish but have eternal life". I don't think the acronym applies to any specific faith as long as they are Christian."

"I can see your point," Tom said, "but what about the acronyms?"

"He was very specific that day, and I can pretty much repeat his message word for word. He said 'let's discuss this one word at a time'."

ALL FEAR of LIFE

Sister Mary began "**ALL** - **A**lways – **L**ove – **L**ife. In life you will undoubtedly have set backs as you go along and hit roadblocks that will frustrate you. Realize that things happen for a reason and it's important to treat every situation as a learning experience. I've found that most things work out if you keep your faith, and the answers seem to appear when we are ready to hear them. If you love life everything is so much easier."

"**FEAR** - **F**alse – **E**vidence – **A**ppearing – **R**eal. Think how often our fears and concerns waste our time and energy. They take our concentration away from what is real, which is our dreams."

"We discussed this with the professor" Tom agreed, "I know I will succeed no matter what."

"That is a great attitude, and it's exactly what I told the Professor. Here is what he told me. We are all afraid of certain things as we go through life, and here are a few things we all fear."

"He did say he was going to cover that with us later!" CC piped in smiling.

Sister Louise added "It made sense when he broke fear down into the six fears we all share at one time or another."

"<u>Poverty</u>. We are all afraid of that. You want to be able to give to the poor, but you don't want to be poor! Correct?"

"We can all agree with that" I said.

"How about <u>Ill Health</u>? Of course, you will get colds, the flu, and upset stomachs. That is not what he was referring to. What you don't want to face are issues like cancer, brain tumors, Parkinson's disease and so forth," she continued, almost sounding like the Professor. It was hard not to agree with her.

Sister Louise could see she was getting through to us, so she continued. "<u>Loss of Love</u>. This can come in a number of ways. It could be a relative or close friend and may be through death or relocation. This is inevitable, but you may also lose someone you fell in love with, either through death or to someone else. The latter can produce negative emotions such as jealousy."

"Then there is <u>Old Age</u>. I know it doesn't seem like it will ever affect you while you are young, but it certainly will. Everyone wants to stay young, in fact one of the most profitable areas of medicine is now plastic surgery. You know it seems like that would never affect you but it certainly will. Did you know that one of the biggest growing and money producing procedures in the medical field is now plastic surgery? No matter how young you look, you will feel the effects of age, and people fear that."

Sister Margaret then spoke, it was amazing to see how they had all adopted the Professor's philosophies. "Let's talk about <u>Death</u>. Nobody wants to die, in fact, most of us don't even like to talk about it. The Professor taught us to live our lives based on what you want someone to say during your eulogy."

"He told us that, too!" I said. "It really makes you think about your actions."

"The last is <u>Criticism</u>. It's hard to believe, but many people are more worried about criticism than death. We are concerned about what people will say or how they would respond if we made a mistake or fail at something. Please understand, failure is not failure unless you accept it as such and stop trying."

"That is hard to disagree with, can I assume 'life' is an acronym too?" Lynn asked with a grin.

"Of course, it is, just like all the Professor's teachings. He taught us the importance of your mindset when things don't go as planned. Or, as he would have said it:"

"**LIFE** – **L**ife – **I**sn't – **F**air – **E**ver, isn't that what we think when things go wrong? We start looking for someone else to blame, instead of taking responsibility for our own attitude. How we respond to everything is found in the MAN."

"The MAN?" I repeated. "This sentence he taught you is getting even crazier than the one he taught us."

"I promise it will make more sense when we get through the whole sentence." Sister Mary reassured us. "In fact, it is the core of happiness and understanding in life."

MAN FROG LIVING A BIBLE

"**MAN** - **M**ental – **A**ttitude – **N**ecessary, rarely do things go exactly as we planned in life. So, it is important to maintain your mental attitude as you encounter both negative and positive things." Sister Louise offered.

"I know, we have to remain positive, and we should not think of negative things as bad, but it's not that easy!" I challenged.

"Very true, but that's not the point she is making. We are talking about the MAN FROG!" The mental attitude that you need to adopt, is the attitude of the 'frog'. It's how we learned to live each and every day?" said Sister Mary.

Sister Louise began again, "**FROG** - **F**ully – **R**ely – **O**n – **G**OD, means that when you experience things, good or bad, you understand that God is giving you that experience for a reason. That doesn't mean you will understand the overall plan, but it does mean you have faith that there is a purpose. Living with that faith, it is difficult not to try and make this a better place for everyone."

"Yes, but aren't we here to have some fun, too? Doesn't God want us to enjoy ourselves while we're here?" Tom asked.

"Of course, your life should be enjoyable, and it gets that way when you help others. You can and should learn to enjoy both your life and the act of helping others." Sister Margaret added.

"**LIVING** – **L**oving – **I**ntelligence – **V**aluing – **I**ntegrity – **N**ear - **G**OD. You know you will be learning as long as you live. Hopefully, you learn from mistakes and avoid repeating them. It helps if you keep your heart near God, so your faith grows along with your skills and abilities," She continued.

"And I bet that's where the 'Bible plays into the acronym." Lynn commented as she finished her ice cream cone.

Sister Mary nodded "Yes indeed, the Bible is important, very important for everyone."

"And I'm sure there's another acronym connected here" I said knowingly.

"By now you certainly should know there is." Sister Mary said laughing.

"**BIBLE – B**asic – **I**nstruction – **B**efore – **L**eaving – **E**arth", Sister Margaret continued, as usual: first the word, then a word representing each letter of the word. "Don't think of the Bible as a book. It is actually over 60 books and they can teach us a lot about how to live, even today. There are a couple of habits that will benefit you greatly. First, read a Bible verse every day, and second, spend a few minutes every morning talking to God about your day. I should add a third, and very important one: when you talk, don't forget to listen! That way, you can end up where you want to be, in Heaven, not where you don't want to be you know, WELL!" as she shrugged her shoulders and giggled.

We were all silent for a moment, wondering how this simple conversation, like many of those with the Professor, had gotten so intense.

"It's not surprising that this sentence ends up talking about faith. I guess that helps us figure out our direction." Lynn said, looking very pleased.

"Well yes and no!" Sister Mary replied. "You see God will show you the way but he won't force you to take it. He wants you to decide where you go in life with the right attitude and focus. You should realize that the way you view LIFE makes all the difference, and this outward demonstration of your faith is what all others can see."

"I get it!" I blurted out. "It's kind of like hiding your light under a basket. It's not much good unless others can see It!"

"Exactly!" Sister Mary beamed. "Now let's continue."

LIFE of FAITH

"**LIFE** - **L**ife - **I**s – **F**ully - **E**xciting, again, it's all in your outlook. We were meant to live fully to our greatest capacity, and to prosper through the use of our talents. We were also meant to experience the world fully through love and even through sorrow and its challenges. It's how we develop into the best person we can be. It's also how we find adventure, opportunity, joy and also how we face the challenges in our lives. Just look back and you'll see that your greatest periods of growth and learning occurred because of difficulties you encountered and overcame. God grants us the gift and the responsibility to choose how each thing or event will affect us. My own experience tells me that the best way to respond is with faith."

"**FAITH** - **F**ind - **A**nswers - **I**n - **T**he - **H**eart, once you discover your true passion in life, it is easier to find your purpose and direction. Your heart can guide you through some very difficult decisions. If you expect an easy path with a shining goal at the end, I'm afraid you will be very disappointed. You may stumble, take the wrong turn, and become discouraged, but if you can keep your faith you will succeed. Becoming a nun was incredibly difficult at times, but each of us would do it all again." All three sisters nodded.

"You are right, sisters. I can see how it could take a lifetime to work out all the meaning in that sentence." Lynn sighed.

I hadn't realized it, but I had been holding my breath as well.

"Oh, we haven't got it all worked out yet," Sister Margaret laughed, "but we are making progress."

"How about giving us a few more hints about what you've learned." Tom prodded.

"Let me answer that with a question." Sister Louise said. "When do you pray?"

Tom fidgeted, not used to such a direct personal question. "Well, um, I guess when I need help."

"And what do you say?" Sister Louise pressed her point.

"Um, I guess I kind of beg for help." Tom admitted, clearly uncomfortable with this line of questioning.

"I have a suggestion," Sister Louise continued. "Try talking to God every day, and instead of immediately asking for help, try starting each conversation with a 'Thank You' for everything you have been given. Some people call it an 'attitude of gratitude'."

"Look at it another way." Sister Mary said. "You each know someone who always seems to be in need of your help. Everything for them is a crisis, and you only hear from them when they need something. You probably even cringe slightly when you see them coming."

We each had someone like that in our lives.

"You also probably have a good friend who you see and talk to regularly, a person who is pleasant, fun to be around and willing to help others." Sister Mary paused and looked at each of us in turn.

We looked at each other and smiled.

"Do they even have to tell you when they need help? Don't you look for ways to make things easier for them? When they are grateful, don't you want to help even more? What makes you think God would be any different?"

Sister Mary knew she had made her point. She would have been great in sales. Then she closed this sale with "Try it for thirty days and see if it doesn't make a difference. What do you have to lose?"

None of us said a thing, but I knew we would give it a try. It was Sister Margaret who broke the silence.

"You all seem to be determined to succeed, and I don't doubt that you will, so let me offer a little guidance. The best way to show your gratitude for all you have been given is to share with others, not just financially, but share yourself. Demonstrate your faith through your actions, as the Professor used to say."

"It's obvious that we are talking about the same Professor," I said. "Would you like to join us in his office tomorrow afternoon?"

"Actually, I stopped at the school last week and went to where his office used to be, but he wasn't there." Sister Margaret sighed.

"In the School of Business building?" Lynn asked.

Sister Margaret nodded.

"Through the entrance, to the right and up on the third floor?" Tom pursued.

All three nodded.

"We could meet there tomorrow with him. I'm sure he'd love to see you." I offered. I really wanted to be part of this meeting.

"We will be at the church after mass tomorrow, but if you call and tell us he is in, we'll be right over." Sister Margaret smiled slightly.

"Do you know something we don't?" Lynn asked.

"I would hope so after all this time." Sister Margaret laughed. "It has been a pleasure meeting the three of you and thanks for the ice cream. Please stay in touch. It's pretty obvious why you received special guidance from the Professor." She gave us each a hug and the three of them walked away.

Tom spoke first. "The Professor will be shocked when we tell him about this tomorrow morning. Let's meet around 8:30."

EPILOGUE

When the three of us arrived at the college the next morning to see the Professor, we went to the third floor as usual. For the first time, there was a receptionist at the desk, and the door to the office was closed.

"Can I help you?" she asked.

"We'd like to see the Professor" I said.

"Did you have an appointment?" she inquired.

"Not exactly, but he told us to stop by any time." I replied.

"Let me see if Professor Ketner is available" she said, picking up the phone.

"Um, we wanted to see Professor Sooncrae!" Lynn corrected.

"You must have the wrong office", she said, looking puzzled. "Professor Ketner has been in this office for nearly 18 years. I've been the receptionist here every day for the last three years and I don't think I've ever heard of Professor Sooncrae, but let me check with Professor Ketner and see if he if he knows… Professor Sooncrae, was it?"

She went into the office, then came back out and motioned us to enter. The tall man seated behind the desk was much older than 60, definitely not the Professor we knew.

"Welcome, my name is Professor Ketner, and I am more than a little confused by your request. I am certainly not aware of a Professor Sooncrae that has ever been in this office or even at this school."

Tom was trying to make sense of all this. "Most people just call him 'Professor', and we've been visiting him here for the past several months."

Professor Ketner was talking again, but none of us actually heard him. We were stunned as we looked around the office. Yes, the library and the ladder were there, but the spiral staircase, the backgammon table and the fantastic desk were missing. It was furnished with standard office furniture, nice, but the magic was gone. When we realized he was talking, he was in mid-sentence.

"…very interesting, though I guess it's not the first time this has happened. There are three nuns who stop by occasionally and they usually just stick their heads in, say 'hello', nod and leave. I think they mentioned something about a spiral staircase, a dart tunnel and a beautiful desk. Actually, they looked almost as confused as you three, and seemed very disappointed not to find what they were looking for. I'm sorry I can't help you. I'm not sure where you were, but it couldn't have been this office. I've been in this office for nearly two decades and the building is actually named after my father, so I've been around campus even longer than that."

We thanked him for seeing us, then stumbled out of the office in a daze. We wandered down the stairs where Lynn and I dropped into the red leather chairs in the atrium, while Tom sat on the couch facing us. "What in the world just happened to us?" I asked.

"I have no idea, this is the most bizarre experience in my life!" Lynn replied.

Tom was looking down at the floor with his head in his hands. When he raised his head, his eyes widened and he said "I don't know about you, but I feel like I've just been given a special blessing," he said as a grin spread across his face.

"What are you talking about?" Lynn and I said in unison.

"Turn around and look at that," he gestured. "Something tells me it's for all of us."

When we turned and looked, there was a small end table with a vase on it. The vase held three roses and a daily quote. My eyes welled up with tears as I read the quote:

Today's Math

1 Cross + 3 Nails = 4 Given.

"I think you're right, Tom, it's a special blessing indeed. I took one of the roses then offered one to Tom and the other to Lynn. Nothing more was said as we linked arms and walked out of the building.

ACKNOWLEDGEMENTS

First of all, I thank God that I am still on this earth. I certainly hope I learn to understand why; and somehow, through this book or otherwise, touch the people I am supposed to touch.

Thanks to Arlene my wife, my love, my life. She has certainly stuck with our vows in marriage and stuck with me through good times and extremely rough times as our life together moved along. She is a strong, loving, and patient woman.

Thanks to Ashley, Kayla, and Sam. It is hard to believe they are all adults on their own now, and the incredible support they are in my life, more now than ever. They are three of the most beautiful, loving human beings that burst my pride daily.

Thanks to Dave Sheely my official editor this time around. He was kind enough to review the previous books as well! He has been a tremendous support and guidance throughout my life on many avenues. He has given me more positive support than any other person. Yes Dave, I am still jumping with my cape!

A special thanks to Margaret Lee, she is the person who encouraged me to start writing again. She is one of the best in our business and a great person to learn from.

Thanks to Herman Lynch who got this ball rolling with a bet on who would be further along in a new book at the end of the year. Herman, looks like you owe me a glass of wine!

Thanks to Blaine Mullis my final proof reader. He did an amazing job picking up on spelling, and punctuation. Also, he redirected my thoughts on some of the dialog to make the read more helpful and positive.

Printed in the United States
By Bookmasters